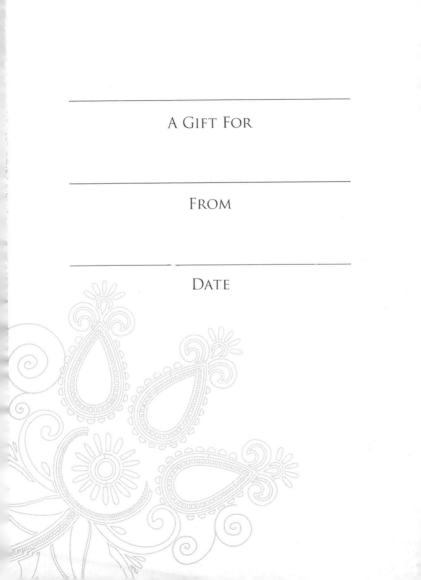

A GIFT FOR

FROM

DATE

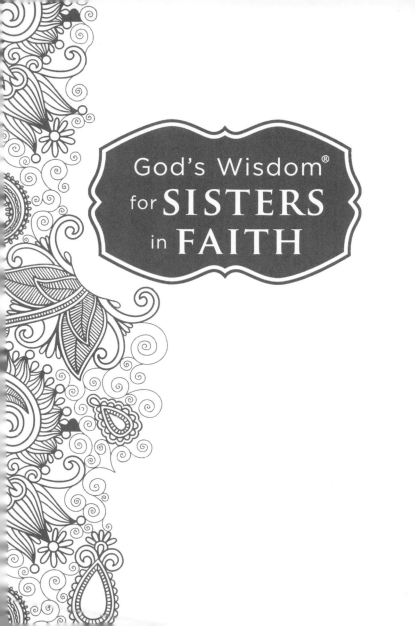

God's Wisdom® for SISTERS in FAITH

God's Wisdom® for SISTERS in FAITH

Sisters in Faith material selected by
MICHELE CLARK JENKINS
STEPHANIE PERRY MOORE

Scripture selected by
JACK COUNTRYMAN

A Division of Thomas Nelson Publishers

THOMAS NELSON
Since 1798

NASHVILLE   DALLAS   MEXICO CITY   RIO DE JANEIRO

Published in Nashville, Tennessee, by Thomas Nelson. Thomas Nelson is a registered trademark of Thomas Nelson, Inc.

Section introductions are taken from the *Sisters in Faith Holy Bible*.

God's Wisdom is a registered trademark of Thomas Nelson.

Thomas Nelson, Inc., titles may be purchased in bulk for educational, business, fund-raising, or sales promotional use. For information, please e-mail SpecialMarkets@ ThomasNelson.com.

Scripture quotations are taken from the KING JAMES VERSION of the Bible.

ISBN-13: 978-1-4003-2253-4

Printed in China

13 14 15 16 17 RRD 6 5 4 3 2 1

CONTENTS

GOD WALKS WITH A SISTER IN FAITH TO . . .

GOD TEACHES A SISTER IN FAITH HOW TO . . .

GOD ENCOURAGES A SISTER IN FAITH TO . . .

GOD CROWNS A SISTER IN FAITH WITH . . .

GOD DELIGHTS IN A SISTER IN FAITH WHO . . .

GOD GIVES A SISTER IN FAITH . . .

Dear Sister in Faith,

God has so richly blessed each of us. But we are assured that on our pilgrimage in this life, trouble *will* come. When that trouble does come, our greatest weapon against the devourer is the Word of God, which exposes the truth of our lives, strengthens our resolve to follow God, and helps us get from glory to glory and from faith to faith in him.

God says in Jeremiah 29:11, "For I know the thoughts that I think toward you, saith the Lord, thoughts of peace, and not of evil, to give you an expected end." We want you, our sister, to know that you are not alone in the battlefield. Christ stands beside you, and so do we, bound to you as your sisters in faith. We love you, and we bless your life. We pray for you and ask God to reveal himself to you day by day and moment by moment.

With blessings and honor,
Michele Clark Jenkins
Stephanie Perry Moore
General Editors

GOD'S WISDOM . . .

FOR A THIRSTY SOUL

O God, thou art my God; early will I seek thee:
My soul thirsteth for thee, my flesh longeth
*   for thee*
in a dry and thirsty land, where no water is.

PSALM 63:1

David, the shepherd boy who became king of Israel, had a vibrant relationship with God, and this verse gives us a glimpse as to why. In the ups and downs and twists and turns of his life, he had one constant—prayer. But it wasn't out of mechanical obligation. It stemmed from a deep understanding that he *needed* God. His flesh longed for God; his very soul thirsted for him. He couldn't wait to seek him out; he couldn't afford to wait. David sought the Lord first thing so that all else could be ordered aright; he sought him as a way of life.

We might be inclined to run to God in times of trouble, when we feel weak and vulnerable. But we cultivate a strong relationship only when we recognize our constant need of him. The truth is, whether we know it or not, our flesh is always weak and vulnerable. And we live in a "dry and thirsty land" (Psalm 63:1) in which we're promised to always have trouble (John 16:33). But prayer keeps us connected to power, grace, joy, and peace. Prayer helps us to abide daily in the Lord. Prayer reminds us that though people let us down, there is One who will never leave us nor forsake us (Hebrews 13:5). Prayer focuses our hearts and minds on what truly matters. When our prayer life becomes as natural as breathing, we can't help but walk in victory.

～～ PRACTICAL APPLICATION ～～

With so many demands on our time, a vibrant prayer life can fall by the wayside. But it's not about setting aside the same number of minutes at the same time every day. Prayer simply means talking to God, anytime, anyplace. No matter the circumstance, turn to him. He's waiting.

～～ PRAYER ～～

Lord, thank you for inviting us to run to your throne of grace. Cultivate in me the precious habit of prayer, that I may maintain a strong relationship with you.

—Kim Cash Tate

Is Really Needed

Get wisdom, get understanding: forget it not;
  neither decline from the words of my
  mouth.
Forsake her not, and she shall preserve thee:
  love her, and she shall keep thee.
Wisdom is the principal thing; therefore
  get wisdom: and with all thy getting get
  understanding.
Exalt her, and she shall promote thee: she shall
  bring thee to honour, when thou dost
  embrace her.
She shall give to thine head an ornament of
  grace: a crown of glory shall she deliver to
  thee.

PROVERBS 4:5–9

Let not mercy and truth forsake thee: bind
them about thy neck; write them upon the
table of thine heart:
So shalt thou find favour and good understanding in the sight of God and man.

PROVERBS 3:3–4

Wisdom hath builded her house, she hath
hewn out her seven pillars:
She hath killed her beasts; she hath mingled
her wine; she hath also furnished her table.
She hath sent forth her maidens: she crieth
upon the highest places of the city,
Whoso is simple, let him turn in hither: as for
him that wanteth understanding, she saith
to him,
Come, eat of my bread, and drink of the wine
which I have mingled.
Forsake the foolish, and live; and go in the way
of understanding.

PROVERBS 9:1–6

Be not wise in thine own eyes: fear the LORD,
and depart from evil.
It shall be health to thy navel, and marrow to
thy bones.

PROVERBS 3:7–8

Walk in wisdom toward them that are without, redeeming the time. Let your speech be always with grace, seasoned with salt, that ye may know how ye ought to answer every man.

COLOSSIANS 4:5–6

Incline thine ear unto wisdom, and apply thine
heart to understanding;
Yea, if thou criest after knowledge, and liftest
up thy voice for understanding;
If thou seekest her as silver, and searchest for
her as for hid treasures;
Then shalt thou understand the fear of the
LORD, and find the knowledge of God.

PROVERBS 2:2–5

If any of you lack wisdom, let him ask of God, that giveth to all men liberally, and upbraideth not; and it shall be given him.

But let him ask in faith, nothing wavering. For he that wavereth is like a wave of the sea driven with the wind and tossed.

JAMES 1:5–6

Thou wilt keep him in perfect peace, whose
    mind is stayed on thee: because he trusteth
    in thee.
Trust ye in the LORD for ever: for in the LORD
    JEHOVAH is everlasting strength.

ISAIAH 26:3–4

Except the LORD build the house, they labour
    in vain that build it: except the LORD keep
    the city, the watchman waketh but in vain.

PSALM 127:1

IS REQUIRED

For the LORD giveth wisdom: out of his mouth
　　cometh knowledge and understanding.
He layeth up sound wisdom for the righteous:
　　he is a buckler to them that walk uprightly.
He keepeth the paths of judgment, and
　　preserveth the way of his saints.
Then shalt thou understand righteousness,
　　and judgment, and equity; yea, every good
　　path.

PROVERBS 2:6–9

How much better is it to get wisdom than
　　gold! and to get understanding rather to be
　　chosen than silver!

PROVERBS 16:16

Doth not wisdom cry? and understanding put
forth her voice? . . .

Unto you, O men, I call; and my voice is to the
sons of man.

O ye simple, understand wisdom: and, ye fools,
be ye of an understanding heart.

Hear; for I will speak of excellent things; and
the opening of my lips shall be right things.

For my mouth shall speak truth; and
wickedness is an abomination to my lips.

All the words of my mouth are in
righteousness; there is nothing froward or
perverse in them.

They are all plain to him that understandeth,
and right to them that find knowledge.

Receive my instruction, and not silver; and
knowledge rather than choice gold.

For wisdom is better than rubies; and all the
things that may be desired are not to be
compared to it.

PROVERBS 8:1, 4–11

I wisdom dwell with prudence, and find out
knowledge of witty inventions.
The fear of the LORD is to hate evil: pride,
and arrogancy, and the evil way, and the
froward mouth, do I hate.
Counsel is mine, and sound wisdom: I am
understanding; I have strength.

PROVERBS 8:12–14

Let no man deceive himself. If any man among you seemeth to be wise in this world, let him become a fool, that he may be wise.

For the wisdom of this world is foolishness with God. For it is written, He taketh the wise in their own craftiness.

And again, The Lord knoweth the thoughts of the wise, that they are vain.

1 CORINTHIANS 3:18–20

For God giveth to a man that is good in his sight wisdom, and knowledge, and joy: but to the sinner he giveth travail, to gather and to heap up, that he may give to him that is good before God. This also is vanity and vexation of spirit.

ECCLESIASTES 2:26

But the salvation of the righteous is of the
    LORD: he is their strength in the time of
    trouble.
And the LORD shall help them, and deliver
    them: he shall deliver them from the
    wicked, and save them, because they trust
    in him.

PSALM 37:39–40

MUST BE FOUND

When wisdom entereth into thine heart, and
knowledge is pleasant unto thy soul;
Discretion shall preserve thee, understanding
shall keep thee:
To deliver thee from the way of the evil man,
from the man that speaketh froward
things.

PROVERBS 2:10–12

Through wisdom is an house builded; and by
understanding it is established:
And by knowledge shall the chambers be filled
with all precious and pleasant riches.

PROVERBS 24:3–4

I love them that love me; and those that seek
me early shall find me.
Riches and honour are with me; yea, durable
riches and righteousness.
My fruit is better than gold, yea, than fine gold;
and my revenue than choice silver.
I lead in the way of righteousness, in the midst
of the paths of judgment:
That I may cause those that love me to inherit
substance; and I will fill their treasures.

PROVERBS 8:17–21

The heart of the righteous studieth to answer:
but the mouth of the wicked poureth out
evil things.

PROVERBS 15:28

Let my mouth be filled with thy praise and
with thy honour all the day.

PSALM 71:8

Say unto wisdom, Thou art my sister; and call
understanding thy kinswoman.

PROVERBS 7:4

O God, thou art my God; early will I seek thee:
my soul thirsteth for thee, my flesh longeth
for thee in a dry and thirsty land, where no
water is.

PSALM 63:1

Is Essential to Succeeding

Happy is the man that findeth wisdom, and
   the man that getteth understanding.
For the merchandise of it is better than the
   merchandise of silver, and the gain thereof
   than fine gold.
She is more precious than rubies: and all the
   things thou canst desire are not to be
   compared unto her.
Length of days is in her right hand; and in her
   left hand riches and honour.
Her ways are ways of pleasantness, and all her
   paths are peace.
She is a tree of life to them that lay hold upon
   her: and happy is every one that retaineth
   her.

Proverbs 3:13–18

Wisdom and knowledge shall be the stability of thy times, and strength of salvation: the fear of the LORD is his treasure.

ISAIAH 33:6

Eat thou honey, because it is good; and the
    honeycomb, which is sweet to thy taste:
So shall the knowledge of wisdom be unto thy
    soul: when thou hast found it, then there
    shall be a reward, and thy expectation shall
    not be cut off.

PROVERBS 24:13–14

Turn you at my reproof: behold, I will pour out
    my spirit unto you, I will make known my
    words unto you.

PROVERBS 1:23

Look to yourselves, that we lose not those things which we have wrought, but that we receive a full reward.

2 JOHN v. 8

Now therefore hearken unto me, O ye children:
for blessed are they that keep my ways.
Hear instruction, and be wise, and refuse it
not.
Blessed is the man that heareth me, watching
daily at my gates, waiting at the posts of
my doors.
For whoso findeth me findeth life, and shall
obtain favour of the LORD.

PROVERBS 8:32–35

For I was ashamed to require of the king a band of soldiers and horsemen to help us against the enemy in the way: because we had spoken unto the king, saying, The hand of our God is upon all them for good that seek him; but his power and his wrath is against all them that forsake him.

EZRA 8:22

But seek ye first the kingdom of God, and his righteousness; and all these things shall be added unto you.

MATTHEW 6:33

Come unto me, all ye that labour and are heavy laden, and I will give you rest.

Take my yoke upon you, and learn of me; for I am meek and lowly in heart: and ye shall find rest unto your souls.

For my yoke is easy, and my burden is light.

MATTHEW 11:28–30

How sweet are thy words unto my taste! yea,
　　sweeter than honey to my mouth!
Through thy precepts I get understanding:
　　therefore I hate every false way.

PSALM 119:103–104

Is Necessary

The simple inherit folly: but the prudent are
crowned with knowledge.

PROVERBS 14:18

The heart of the prudent getteth knowledge;
and the ear of the wise seeketh knowledge.

PROVERBS 18:15

A fool despiseth his father's instruction: but he
that regardeth reproof is prudent.

PROVERBS 15:5

House and riches are the inheritance of fathers:
and a prudent wife is from the LORD.

PROVERBS 19:14

The wise in heart shall be called prudent:
and the sweetness of the lips increaseth
learning.

PROVERBS 16:21

Wise men lay up knowledge: but the mouth of
the foolish is near destruction.

PROVERBS 10:14

For this cause we also, since the day we heard
it, do not cease to pray for you, and to desire that
ye might be filled with the knowledge of his will
in all wisdom and spiritual understanding;

That ye might walk worthy of the Lord unto
all pleasing, being fruitful in every good work,
and increasing in the knowledge of God.

COLOSSIANS 1:9–10

GOD DRAWS CLOSE TO A SISTER IN FAITH WHO . . .

HAS FAITH IN GOD

Here's a secret: mommies' beds are powerful. When my kids snuggled in bed with me, colds were cured, bad days got better, tears dried up, and no creepy thing or bump in the night stood a chance! For my kids, life was right in my presence.

Sisters, life is right when we snuggle in God's presence. Moses understood this powerful principle better than anyone. In Exodus 33:15, he said to the Lord, "If thy presence go not with me [to the promised land], carry us not up hence." In essence, Moses was saying to God: "Daddy, we don't feel safe without you, and we aren't going to do life without you." He flat-out refused to leave God's presence. And so should we.

In our day-to-day lives as women, we often feel that we have to have the answers, we have to manage our homes, we have to take care of everyone's needs, and honestly, it's just too easy to forget that we are God's children. Moses didn't forget that there is safety, provision, comfort, and peace in God's presence. When you have faith in God, you can run to his presence in times of trouble, just like my little ones ran to me.

It's time that we as believers run to our God, putting complete faith and confidence in him. Have you had any bad days recently? Then lift your hands right now and get into God's presence. Have there been tears, scary situations, or bumps in the night that have left you feeling vulnerable, afraid, lonely, or fearful? Then know that your heavenly Father is waiting right now, a warm spot right next to him, for you to snuggle close in his presence. Life will be so right when you do.

—Jennifer Keitt

LIFTS UP HOLY HANDS

I will bless the LORD at all times: his praise
    shall continually be in my mouth.
My soul shall make her boast in the LORD: the
    humble shall hear thereof, and be glad.
O magnify the LORD with me, and let us exalt
    his name together.
I sought the LORD, and he heard me, and
    delivered me from all my fears.

PSALM 34:1–4

Favour is deceitful, and beauty is vain: but a
    woman that feareth the LORD, she shall be
    praised.
Give her of the fruit of her hands; and let her
    own works praise her in the gates.

PROVERBS 31:30–31

And they rose early in the morning, and went forth into the wilderness of Tekoa: and as they went forth, Jehoshaphat stood and said, Hear me, O Judah, and ye inhabitants of Jerusalem; Believe in the LORD your God, so shall ye be established; believe his prophets, so shall ye prosper.

And when he had consulted with the people, he appointed singers unto the LORD, and that should praise the beauty of holiness, as they went out before the army, and to say, Praise the LORD; for his mercy endureth for ever.

2 CHRONICLES 20:20–21

Let them shout for joy, and be glad, that favour
    my righteous cause: yea, let them say
    continually, Let the LORD be magnified,
    which hath pleasure in the prosperity of his
    servant.
And my tongue shall speak of thy righteous-
    ness and of thy praise all the day long.

PSALM 35:27–28

Praise ye the LORD. Praise the LORD, O my
soul.

While I live will I praise the LORD: I will sing
praises unto my God while I have any
being.

Put not your trust in princes, nor in the son of
man, in whom there is no help.

His breath goeth forth, he returneth to his
earth; in that very day his thoughts perish.

Happy is he that hath the God of Jacob for his
help, whose hope is in the LORD his God:

Which made heaven, and earth, the sea, and
all that therein is: which keepeth truth for
ever:

Which executeth judgment for the oppressed:
which giveth food to the hungry. The LORD
looseth the prisoners:

The LORD openeth the eyes of the blind: the
LORD raiseth them that are bowed down:
the LORD loveth the righteous:

The LORD preserveth the strangers; he relieveth

the fatherless and widow: but the way of the
   wicked he turneth upside down.
The LORD shall reign for ever, even thy God,
   O Zion, unto all generations. Praise ye the
   LORD.

PSALM 146

Praise ye the LORD. Praise God in his
   sanctuary: praise him in the firmament of
   his power.
Praise him for his mighty acts: praise him
   according to his excellent greatness.
Praise him with the sound of the trumpet:
   praise him with the psaltery and harp.
Praise him with the timbrel and dance: praise
   him with stringed instruments and organs.
Praise him upon the loud cymbals: praise him
   upon the high sounding cymbals.
Let every thing that hath breath praise the
   LORD. Praise ye the LORD.

PSALM 150

PUTS HER TRUST IN HIM

Trust in the LORD with all thine heart; and
    lean not unto thine own understanding.
In all thy ways acknowledge him, and he shall
    direct thy paths.

PROVERBS 3:5–6

Lift up your eyes on high, and behold who
hath created these things, that bringeth out their
host by number: he calleth them all by names by
the greatness of his might, for that he is strong in
power; not one faileth.

ISAIAH 40:26

Great is our Lord, and of great power: his
    understanding is infinite.

PSALM 147:5

As for God, his way is perfect: the word of the
LORD is tried: he is a buckler to all those
that trust in him.

PSALM 18:30

But in all things approving ourselves as the
ministers of God, in much patience, in afflic-
tions, in necessities, in distresses. . . .

By pureness, by knowledge, by long suffering, by kindness, by the Holy Ghost, by love
unfeigned,

By the word of truth, by the power of God,
by the armour of righteousness on the right hand
and on the left.

2 CORINTHIANS 6:4, 6–7

What time I am afraid, I will trust in thee.
In God I will praise his word, in God I have put
my trust; I will not fear what flesh can do
unto me.

PSALM 56:3–4

The LORD is my rock, and my fortress, and my
    deliverer; my God, my strength, in whom I
    will trust; my buckler, and the horn of my
    salvation, and my high tower.
I will call upon the LORD, who is worthy to
    be praised: so shall I be saved from mine
    enemies.

PSALM 18:2–3

In thee, O LORD, do I put my trust: let me
    never be put to confusion.
Deliver me in thy righteousness, and cause me
    to escape: incline thine ear unto me, and
    save me.
Be thou my strong habitation, whereunto I
    may continually resort: thou hast given
    commandment to save me; for thou art my
    rock and my fortress.

PSALM 71:1–3

He giveth power to the faint; and to them
that have no might he increaseth strength.

ISAIAH 40:29

For God hath not given us the spirit of fear;
but of power, and of love, and of a sound mind.

2 TIMOTHY 1:7

Thou wilt keep him in perfect peace, whose
    mind is stayed on thee: because he trusteth
    in thee.
Trust ye in the LORD for ever: for in the LORD
    JEHOVAH is everlasting strength.

ISAIAH 26:3–4

ABIDES IN HIS LOVE

And thou shalt love the LORD thy God with all thine heart, and with all thy soul, and with all thy might.

And these words, which I command thee this day, shall be in thine heart:

And thou shalt teach them diligently unto thy children, and shalt talk of them when thou sittest in thine house, and when thou walkest by the way, and when thou liest down, and when thou risest up.

And thou shalt bind them for a sign upon thine hand, and they shall be as frontlets between thine eyes.

DEUTERONOMY 6:5–8

Who shall separate us from the love of Christ? shall tribulation, or distress, or persecution, or famine, or nakedness, or peril, or sword? . . .

For I am persuaded, that neither death, nor life, nor angels, nor principalities, nor powers, nor things present, nor things to come,

Nor height, nor depth, nor any other creature, shall be able to separate us from the love of God, which is in Christ Jesus our Lord.

ROMANS 8:35, 38–39

And hereby we do know that we know him, if we keep his commandments.

He that saith, I know him, and keepeth not his commandments, is a liar, and the truth is not in him.

But whoso keepeth his word, in him verily is the love of God perfected: hereby know we that we are in him.

He that saith he abideth in him ought himself also so to walk, even as he walked.

1 JOHN 2:3–6

O love the LORD, all ye his saints: for the LORD
   preserveth the faithful, and plentifully
   rewardeth the proud doer.
Be of good courage, and he shall strengthen
   your heart, all ye that hope in the LORD.

PSALM 31:23–24

If ye love me, keep my commandments.

And I will pray the Father, and he shall give you another Comforter, that he may abide with you for ever;

Even the Spirit of truth; whom the world cannot receive, because it seeth him not, neither knoweth him: but ye know him; for he dwelleth with you, and shall be in you.

I will not leave you comfortless: I will come to you.

JOHN 14:15–18

For this cause I bow my knees unto the Father of our Lord Jesus Christ,

Of whom the whole family in heaven and earth is named,

That he would grant you, according to the riches of his glory, to be strengthened with might by his Spirit in the inner man;

That Christ may dwell in your hearts by faith; that ye, being rooted and grounded in love,

May be able to comprehend with all saints what is the breadth, and length, and depth, and height;

And to know the love of Christ, which passeth knowledge, that ye might be filled with all the fulness of God.

Ephesians 3:14–19

PRAYS THAT HIS WILL BE DONE

~~·~~

Verily, verily, I say unto you, He that heareth my word, and believeth on him that sent me, hath everlasting life, and shall not come into condemnation; but is passed from death unto life. . . .

For as the Father hath life in himself; so hath he given to the Son to have life in himself;

And hath given him authority to execute judgment also, because he is the Son of man. . . .

I can of mine own self do nothing: as I hear, I judge: and my judgment is just; because I seek not mine own will, but the will of the Father which hath sent me.

JOHN 5:24, 26–27, 30

Deliver me, O Lord, from mine enemies: I flee
   unto thee to hide me.
Teach me to do thy will; for thou art my God:
   thy spirit is good; lead me into the land of
   uprightness.

Psalm 143:9–10

And he said unto them, When ye pray, say,
Our Father which art in heaven, Hallowed be thy
name. Thy kingdom come. Thy will be done, as
in heaven, so in earth.

Give us day by day our daily bread.

And forgive us our sins; for we also forgive
every one that is indebted to us. And lead us not
into temptation; but deliver us from evil.

Luke 11:2–4

The Lord is far from the wicked: but he
   heareth the prayer of the righteous.

Proverbs 15:29

Is any among you afflicted? let him pray. Is any merry? let him sing psalms.

Is any sick among you? let him call for the elders of the church; and let them pray over him, anointing him with oil in the name of the Lord:

And the prayer of faith shall save the sick, and the Lord shall raise him up; and if he have committed sins, they shall be forgiven him.

Confess your faults one to another, and pray one for another, that ye may be healed. The effectual fervent prayer of a righteous man availeth much.

JAMES 5:13–16

See then that ye walk circumspectly, not as fools, but as wise,

Redeeming the time, because the days are evil.

Wherefore be ye not unwise, but understanding what the will of the Lord is. . . .

Giving thanks always for all things unto God and the Father in the name of our Lord Jesus Christ.

EPHESIANS 5:15–17, 20

For I came down from heaven, not to do mine own will, but the will of him that sent me.

And this is the Father's will which hath sent me, that of all which he hath given me I should lose nothing, but should raise it up again at the last day.

And this is the will of him that sent me, that every one which seeth the Son, and believeth on him, may have everlasting life: and I will raise him up at the last day.

JOHN 6:38–40

For this shall every one that is godly pray unto
    thee in a time when thou mayest be found:
    surely in the floods of great waters they
    shall not come nigh unto him.
Thou art my hiding place; thou shalt preserve
    me from trouble; thou shalt compass me
    about with songs of deliverance. Selah.

PSALM 32:6–7

LETS HIS LIGHT SHINE

Thy word is a lamp unto my feet, and a light
unto my path.
I have sworn, and I will perform it, that I will
keep thy righteous judgments.

PSALM 119:105–106

For ye were sometimes darkness, but now are
ye light in the Lord: walk as children of light:
(For the fruit of the Spirit is in all goodness
and righteousness and truth).

EPHESIANS 5:8–9

I am come a light into the world, that whosoever believeth on me should not abide in
darkness.

JOHN 12:46

Ye are the light of the world. A city that is set on an hill cannot be hid.

Neither do men light a candle, and put it under a bushel, but on a candlestick; and it giveth light unto all that are in the house.

Let your light so shine before men, that they may see your good works, and glorify your Father which is in heaven.

MATTHEW 5:14–16

The light of the body is the eye: therefore when thine eye is single, thy whole body also is full of light; but when thine eye is evil, thy body also is full of darkness.

Take heed therefore that the light which is in thee be not darkness.

If thy whole body therefore be full of light, having no part dark, the whole shall be full of light, as when the bright shining of a candle doth give thee light.

LUKE 11:34–36

O send out thy light and thy truth: let them
    lead me; let them bring me unto thy holy
    hill, and to thy tabernacles.
Then will I go unto the altar of God, unto God
    my exceeding joy: yea, upon the harp will I
    praise thee, O God my God.

PSALM 43:3–4

This then is the message which we have heard of him, and declare unto you, that God is light, and in him is no darkness at all.

If we say that we have fellowship with him, and walk in darkness, we lie, and do not the truth:

But if we walk in the light, as he is in the light, we have fellowship one with another, and the blood of Jesus Christ his Son cleanseth us from all sin.

1 JOHN 1:5–7

REJOICES IN THE LORD ALWAYS

Rejoice in the LORD, O ye righteous: for praise
  is comely for the upright.
Praise the LORD with harp: sing unto him
  with the psaltery and an instrument of ten
  strings.
Sing unto him a new song; play skilfully with a
  loud noise.
For the word of the LORD is right; and all his
  works are done in truth.
He loveth righteousness and judgment: the
  earth is full of the goodness of the LORD.

PSALM 33:1–5

But let the righteous be glad; let them rejoice
before God: yea, let them exceedingly
rejoice.

Sing unto God, sing praises to his name: extol
him that rideth upon the heavens by his
name JAH, and rejoice before him.

PSALM 68:3–4

O worship the LORD in the beauty of holiness:
fear before him, all the earth. . . .

Let the heavens rejoice, and let the earth be
glad; let the sea roar, and the fulness
thereof.

Let the field be joyful, and all that is therein:
then shall all the trees of the wood rejoice

Before the LORD: for he cometh, for he cometh
to judge the earth: he shall judge the world
with righteousness, and the people with his
truth.

PSALM 96:9, 11–13

Verily, verily, I say unto you, That ye shall weep and lament, but the world shall rejoice: and ye shall be sorrowful, but your sorrow shall be turned into joy.

A woman when she is in travail hath sorrow, because her hour is come: but as soon as she is delivered of the child, she remembereth no more the anguish, for joy that a man is born into the world.

And ye now therefore have sorrow: but I will see you again, and your heart shall rejoice, and your joy no man taketh from you.

JOHN 16:20–22

Rejoice in the Lord always: and again I say, Rejoice.
Let your moderation be known unto all men. The Lord is at hand.

PHILIPPIANS 4:4–5

Let love be without dissimulation. Abhor that which is evil; cleave to that which is good.

Be kindly affectioned one to another with brotherly love; in honour preferring one another;

Not slothful in business; fervent in spirit; serving the Lord;

Rejoicing in hope; patient in tribulation; continuing instant in prayer;

Distributing to the necessity of saints; given to hospitality.

Bless them which persecute you: bless, and curse not.

Rejoice with them that do rejoice, and weep with them that weep.

ROMANS 12:9–15

Rejoice evermore.

Pray without ceasing.

In every thing give thanks: for this is the will of God in Christ Jesus concerning you.

1 THESSALONIANS 5:16–18

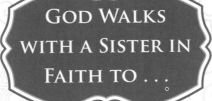

GOD WALKS WITH A SISTER IN FAITH TO . . .

HELP HER FIND GLORY IN WAITING

And not only so, but we glory in tribulations also: knowing that tribulation worketh patience; And patience, experience; and experience, hope: And hope maketh not ashamed; because the love of God is shed abroad in our hearts by the Holy Ghost which is given unto us.

ROMANS 5:3–5

In our microwave, instant-messaging, drive-through, cell-phone world, one thing many of us are not great at is patience. More succinctly: we hate to wait. Yet in reality, many of us hurry up to wait. We want what we want and we want it yesterday!

When going through tribulations, we naturally want our trials to be over and done quickly. But let us learn to go through whatever is before us (the good and bad) with joy, knowing that what the enemy may have intended for evil, God can and will use for our good. Glory in the waiting, with the knowledge that, in the end, something good will come.

～ PRACTICAL APPLICATION ～

Troubles, problems, trials, suffering, misfortunes, evil—tribulations have a way of getting our full attention. But we can shout with joy knowing that what may have begun as tribulation works in us patience, especially when we can do nothing *except* wait on God. Out of patience comes experience. Experience? Yes, we experience the true meaning of Isaiah 40:31: "But they that wait upon the LORD shall renew their strength; they shall mount up with wings as eagles; they shall run, and not be weary; and they shall walk, and not faint." And once experience is gained, we then have hope . . . we have history. And that means the next time tribulation rears its head, we won't worry because we know what God can do!

~~ PRAYER ~~

Dear Father, I thank you that no matter what I'm faced with, I can go through it with joy and patience, with full knowledge that you're with me. Through patience, I'm being perfected. I trust you completely, knowing that the love you have for me is shed abroad in my heart and that, no matter what comes along, I'm more than a conqueror through Christ.

—Vanessa Davis Griggs

Heal Her Broken Heart

~·~·~·~

Praise ye the Lord: for it is good to sing praises
    unto our God; for it is pleasant; and praise
    is comely. . . .
He healeth the broken in heart, and bindeth up
    their wounds.
He telleth the number of the stars; he calleth
    them all by their names.
Great is our Lord, and of great power: his
    understanding is infinite.

Psalm 147:1, 3–5

And the Lord shall guide thee continually,
and satisfy thy soul in drought, and make fat thy
bones: and thou shalt be like a watered garden,
and like a spring of water, whose waters fail not.

Isaiah 58:11

Lord, thou hast heard the desire of the
   humble: thou wilt prepare their heart, thou
   wilt cause thine ear to hear:
To judge the fatherless and the oppressed, that
   the man of the earth may no more oppress.

Psalm 10:17–18

The righteous cry, and the Lord heareth, and
   delivereth them out of all their troubles.
The Lord is nigh unto them that are of a
   broken heart; and saveth such as be of a
   contrite spirit.

Psalm 34:17–18

Come unto me, all ye that labour and are
heavy laden, and I will give you rest.

Take my yoke upon you, and learn of me; for
I am meek and lowly in heart: and ye shall find
rest unto your souls.

Matthew 11:28–29

The LORD also will be a refuge for the
    oppressed, a refuge in times of trouble.
And they that know thy name will put their
    trust in thee: for thou, LORD, hast not
    forsaken them that seek thee.

PSALM 9:9–10

I will worship toward thy holy temple, and
    praise thy name for thy lovingkindness and
    for thy truth: for thou hast magnified thy
    word above all thy name.
In the day when I cried thou answeredst me, and
    strengthenedst me with strength in my soul.

PSALM 138:2–3

The Spirit of the Lord GOD is upon me;
because the LORD hath anointed me to preach
good tidings unto the meek; he hath sent me to
bind up the brokenhearted, to proclaim liberty
to the captives, and the opening of the prison to
them that are bound.

ISAIAH 61:1

GIVE HER REST FROM TROUBLE

Blessed is the man whom thou chastenest, O
    LORD, and teachest him out of thy law;
That thou mayest give him rest from the days
    of adversity, until the pit be digged for the
    wicked.

PSALM 94:12–13

A merry heart doeth good like a medicine: but
    a broken spirit drieth the bones.

PROVERBS 17:22

If thou faint in the day of adversity, thy
    strength is small.

PROVERBS 24:10

In the day of prosperity be joyful, but in the day of adversity consider: God also hath set the one over against the other, to the end that man should find nothing after him.

ECCLESIASTES 7:14

Beloved, think it not strange concerning the fiery trial which is to try you, as though some strange thing happened unto you:

But rejoice, inasmuch as ye are partakers of Christ's sufferings; that, when his glory shall be revealed, ye may be glad also with exceeding joy.

1 PETER 4:12–13

Now thanks be unto God, which always causeth us to triumph in Christ, and maketh manifest the savour of his knowledge by us in every place.

For we are unto God a sweet savour of Christ, in them that are saved, and in them that perish.

2 CORINTHIANS 2:14–15

For this thing I besought the Lord thrice, that it might depart from me.

And he said unto me, My grace is sufficient for thee: for my strength is made perfect in weakness. Most gladly therefore will I rather glory in my infirmities, that the power of Christ may rest upon me.

2 CORINTHIANS 12:8–9

GOD WALKS WITH A SISTER
IN FAITH TO . . .

HELP HER BE ANXIOUS
FOR NOTHING

The LORD is high above all nations, and his
glory above the heavens.
Who is like unto the LORD our God, who
dwelleth on high,
Who humbleth himself to behold the things
that are in heaven, and in the earth!
He raiseth up the poor out of the dust, and
lifteth the needy out of the dunghill;
That he may set him with princes, even with
the princes of his people.
He maketh the barren woman to keep house,
and to be a joyful mother of children.
Praise ye the LORD.

PSALM 113:4–9

My soul, wait thou only upon God; for my
    expectation is from him.
He only is my rock and my salvation: he is my
    defence; I shall not be moved.
In God is my salvation and my glory: the rock
    of my strength, and my refuge, is in God.

Psalm 62:5–7

When thou passest through the waters, I will be with thee; and through the rivers, they shall not overflow thee: when thou walkest through the fire, thou shalt not be burned; neither shall the flame kindle upon thee.

For I am the Lord thy God, the Holy One of Israel, thy Saviour: I gave Egypt for thy ransom, Ethiopia and Seba for thee.

Since thou wast precious in my sight, thou hast been honourable, and I have loved thee: therefore will I give men for thee, and people for thy life.

Isaiah 43:2–4

Therefore I say unto you, Take no thought for your life, what ye shall eat, or what ye shall drink; nor yet for your body, what ye shall put on. Is not the life more than meat, and the body than raiment?

Behold the fowls of the air: for they sow not, neither do they reap, nor gather into barns; yet your heavenly Father feedeth them. Are ye not much better than they?

Which of you by taking thought can add one cubit unto his stature?

And why take ye thought for raiment? Consider the lilies of the field, how they grow; they toil not, neither do they spin:

And yet I say unto you, That even Solomon in all his glory was not arrayed like one of these.

Wherefore, if God so clothe the grass of the field, which to day is, and to morrow is cast into the oven, shall he not much more clothe you, O ye of little faith?

Therefore take no thought, saying, What shall we eat? or, What shall we drink? or, Wherewithal shall we be clothed?

(For after all these things do the Gentiles seek:) for your heavenly Father knoweth that ye have need of all these things.

But seek ye first the kingdom of God, and his righteousness; and all these things shall be added unto you.

MATTHEW 6:25–33

Be careful for nothing; but in every thing by prayer and supplication with thanksgiving let your requests be made known unto God.

And the peace of God, which passeth all understanding, shall keep your hearts and minds through Christ Jesus.

PHILIPPIANS 4:6–7

I have called upon thee, for thou wilt hear me,
   O God: incline thine ear unto me, and
   hear my speech.
Shew thy marvellous lovingkindness, O thou
   that savest by thy right hand them which
   put their trust in thee from those that rise
   up against them.
Keep me as the apple of the eye, hide me under
   the shadow of thy wings.

PSALM 17:6–8

GUIDE HER TO WAIT ON THE LORD

But they that wait upon the LORD shall renew their strength; they shall mount up with wings as eagles; they shall run, and not be weary; and they shall walk, and not faint.

ISAIAH 40:31

My brethren, count it all joy when ye fall into divers temptations;

Knowing this, that the trying of your faith worketh patience.

But let patience have her perfect work, that ye may be perfect and entire, wanting nothing.

JAMES 1:2–4

For whatsoever things were written aforetime were written for our learning, that we through patience and comfort of the scriptures might have hope.

Now the God of patience and consolation grant you to be likeminded one toward another according to Christ Jesus:

That ye may with one mind and one mouth glorify God, even the Father of our Lord Jesus Christ.

ROMANS 15:4–6

I wait for the LORD, my soul doth wait, and in
his word do I hope.
My soul waiteth for the Lord more than they
that watch for the morning: I say, more
than they that watch for the morning.

PSALM 130:5–6

I cried unto the LORD with my voice, and he
    heard me out of his holy hill. Selah.
I laid me down and slept; I awaked; for the
    LORD sustained me.

PSALM 3:4–5

Wait on the LORD: be of good courage, and he
    shall strengthen thine heart: wait, I say, on
    the LORD.

PSALM 27:14

Be patient therefore, brethren, unto the coming of the Lord. Behold, the husbandman waiteth for the precious fruit of the earth, and hath long patience for it, until he receive the early and latter rain.

Be ye also patient; stablish your hearts: for the coming of the Lord draweth nigh.

JAMES 5:7–8

LET HER KNOW THAT HE IS A GOOD GOD

~~·~~

But thou, O man of God, flee these things; and follow after righteousness, godliness, faith, love, patience, meekness.

Fight the good fight of faith, lay hold on eternal life, whereunto thou art also called, and hast professed a good profession before many witnesses.

I give thee charge in the sight of God, who quickeneth all things, and before Christ Jesus, who before Pontius Pilate witnessed a good confession;

That thou keep this commandment without spot, unrebukable, until the appearing of our Lord Jesus Christ.

1 TIMOTHY 6:11–14

Lord, I cry unto thee: make haste unto me; give
ear unto my voice, when I cry unto thee.
Let my prayer be set forth before thee as
incense; and the lifting up of my hands as
the evening sacrifice.

PSALM 141:1–2

Who is a wise man and endued with knowledge among you? let him shew out of a good conversation his works with meekness of wisdom. . . .

But the wisdom that is from above is first pure, then peaceable, gentle, and easy to be intreated, full of mercy and good fruits, without partiality, and without hypocrisy.

And the fruit of righteousness is sown in peace of them that make peace.

JAMES 3:13, 17–18

Therefore, brethren, stand fast, and hold the traditions which ye have been taught, whether by word, or our epistle.

Now our Lord Jesus Christ himself, and God, even our Father, which hath loved us, and hath given us everlasting consolation and good hope through grace,

Comfort your hearts, and stablish you in every good word and work.

2 Thessalonians 2:15–17

I know that, whatsoever God doeth, it shall be for ever: nothing can be put to it, nor any thing taken from it: and God doeth it, that men should fear before him.

That which hath been is now; and that which is to be hath already been; and God requireth that which is past.

Ecclesiastes 3:14–15

SIT AT HIS FEET

*And Jesus answered and said unto her,
Martha, Martha, thou art careful and
troubled about many things.*

LUKE 10:41

I was beside myself! Jesus, our Lord, was
coming to our house to teach. My house
needed to be cleaned from top to bottom. I

wondered what I could possibly serve the one who does miracles. There was so much to do as the people arrived, making drinks and bringing food, making everyone comfortable.

I couldn't understand my sister, Mary. She was doing nothing to help me. She was acting like a guest and just sitting down at Jesus' feet. Couldn't she see I needed help in the kitchen?

I finally had had enough! Jesus didn't seem to notice that she wasn't helping me, and he said nothing to her. So I asked him why. I felt so foolish when he cautioned me that rushing around was causing me to miss the purposes for which he had come. I was missing his teaching because of my busyness. I realized that, at times, I should be like my sister and just sit at his feet.

I learned my lesson well, and I've tried to stay focused on my faith. When my brother, Lazarus, died before Jesus could get to him, I still believed that God could and would do all things through Jesus, who is the Messiah. I believed it was not too late for Jesus to save my brother. My faith did not return void—Jesus raised my brother from the dead!

—Michele Clark Jenkins

TRUST IN GOD WITH ALL HER HEART

I will love thee, O LORD, my strength.
The LORD is my rock, and my fortress, and my
    deliverer; my God, my strength, in whom I
    will trust; my buckler, and the horn of my
    salvation, and my high tower.

PSALM 18:1–2

Trust in the LORD with all thine heart; and
    lean not unto thine own understanding.
In all thy ways acknowledge him, and he shall
    direct thy paths.

PROVERBS 3:5–6

The LORD is thy keeper: the LORD is thy shade
upon thy right hand.
The sun shall not smite thee by day, nor the
moon by night.
The LORD shall preserve thee from all evil: he
shall preserve thy soul.
The LORD shall preserve thy going out and thy
coming in from this time forth, and even
for evermore.

PSALM 121:5–8

I will say of the LORD, He is my refuge and my
fortress: my God; in him will I trust.
Surely he shall deliver thee from the snare
of the fowler, and from the noisome
pestilence.
He shall cover thee with his feathers, and
under his wings shalt thou trust: his truth
shall be thy shield and buckler.

PSALM 91:2–4

Bow down thine ear, and hear the words of
the wise, and apply thine heart unto my
knowledge.
For it is a pleasant thing if thou keep them
within thee; they shall withal be fitted in
thy lips.
That thy trust may be in the LORD, I have made
known to thee this day, even to thee.

PROVERBS 22:17–19

Trust in the LORD, and do good; so shalt thou
dwell in the land, and verily thou shalt be
fed.
Delight thyself also in the LORD: and he shall
give thee the desires of thine heart.
Commit thy way unto the LORD; trust also in
him; and he shall bring it to pass.
And he shall bring forth thy righteousness as
the light, and thy judgment as the noonday.

PSALM 37:3–6

But know that the LORD hath set apart him
that is godly for himself: the LORD will
hear when I call unto him.
Stand in awe, and sin not: commune with your
own heart upon your bed, and be still.
Selah.
Offer the sacrifices of righteousness, and put
your trust in the LORD.

PSALM 4:3–5

Have Steadfast Faith

~•~

Wherefore take unto you the whole armour of God, that ye may be able to withstand in the evil day, and having done all, to stand.

Stand therefore, having your loins girt about with truth, and having on the breastplate of righteousness;

And your feet shod with the preparation of the gospel of peace;

Above all, taking the shield of faith, wherewith ye shall be able to quench all the fiery darts of the wicked.

And take the helmet of salvation, and the sword of the Spirit, which is the word of God

EPHESIANS 6:13–17

Let us draw near with a true heart in full assurance of faith, having our hearts sprinkled from an evil conscience, and our bodies washed with pure water.

Let us hold fast the profession of our faith without wavering; (for he is faithful that promised).

HEBREWS 10:22–23

But without faith it is impossible to please him: for he that cometh to God must believe that he is, and that he is a rewarder of them that diligently seek him.

HEBREWS 11:6

Have not I commanded thee? Be strong and of a good courage; be not afraid, neither be thou dismayed: for the LORD thy God is with thee whithersoever thou goest.

JOSHUA 1:9

Now he that hath wrought us for the self-same thing is God, who also hath given unto us the earnest of the Spirit.

Therefore we are always confident, knowing that, whilst we are at home in the body, we are absent from the Lord:

(For we walk by faith, not by sight.)

2 CORINTHIANS 5:5–7

Beloved, when I gave all diligence to write unto you of the common salvation, it was needful for me to write unto you, and exhort you that ye should earnestly contend for the faith which was once delivered unto the saints. . . .

But ye, beloved, building up yourselves on your most holy faith, praying in the Holy Ghost,

Keep yourselves in the love of God, looking for the mercy of our Lord Jesus Christ unto eternal life.

JUDE VV. 3, 20–21

Wherefore seeing we also are compassed about with so great a cloud of witnesses, let us lay aside every weight, and the sin which doth so easily beset us, and let us run with patience the race that is set before us,

Looking unto Jesus the author and finisher of our faith; who for the joy that was set before him endured the cross, despising the shame, and is set down at the right hand of the throne of God.

HEBREWS 12:1–2

Therefore, my beloved brethren, be ye stedfast, unmoveable, always abounding in the work of the Lord, forasmuch as ye know that your labour is not in vain in the Lord.

1 CORINTHIANS 15:58

PUT GOD FIRST

~·~·~·~

For the grace of God that bringeth salvation hath appeared to all men,

Teaching us that, denying ungodliness and worldly lusts, we should live soberly, righteously, and godly, in this present world;

Looking for that blessed hope, and the glorious appearing of the great God and our Saviour Jesus Christ;

Who gave himself for us, that he might redeem us from all iniquity, and purify unto himself a peculiar people, zealous of good works.

TITUS 2:11–14

Create in me a clean heart, O God; and renew a
   right spirit within me.
Cast me not away from thy presence; and take
   not thy holy spirit from me.
Restore unto me the joy of thy salvation; and
   uphold me with thy free spirit.
Then will I teach transgressors thy ways; and
   sinners shall be converted unto thee.
Deliver me from bloodguiltiness, O God, thou
   God of my salvation: and my tongue shall
   sing aloud of thy righteousness.

PSALM 51:10–14

I am crucified with Christ: nevertheless I
live; yet not I, but Christ liveth in me: and the life
which I now live in the flesh I live by the faith of
the Son of God, who loved me, and gave himself
for me.

GALATIANS 2:20

The tongue of the wise useth knowledge
aright: but the mouth of fools poureth out
foolishness.
The eyes of the Lord are in every place,
beholding the evil and the good.
A wholesome tongue is a tree of life: but
perverseness therein is a breach in the
spirit.

Proverbs 15:2–4

Let the word of Christ dwell in you richly
in all wisdom; teaching and admonishing one
another in psalms and hymns and spiritual
songs, singing with grace in your hearts to the
Lord.

And whatsoever ye do in word or deed, do all
in the name of the Lord Jesus, giving thanks to
God and the Father by him.

Colossians 3:16–17

Because thy lovingkindness is better than life,
my lips shall praise thee.
Thus will I bless thee while I live: I will lift up
my hands in thy name.
My soul shall be satisfied as with marrow and
fatness; and my mouth shall praise thee
with joyful lips:
When I remember thee upon my bed, and
meditate on thee in the night watches.
Because thou hast been my help, therefore in
the shadow of thy wings will I rejoice.
My soul followeth hard after thee: thy right
hand upholdeth me.

PSALM 63:3–8

REST UNDER THE SHELTER OF HIS WING

The LORD is thy keeper: the LORD is thy shade
upon thy right hand.
The sun shall not smite thee by day, nor the
moon by night.
The LORD shall preserve thee from all evil: he
shall preserve thy soul.
The LORD shall preserve thy going out and thy
coming in from this time forth, and even
for evermore.

PSALM 121:5–8

But whoso hearkeneth unto me shall dwell
safely, and shall be quiet from fear of evil.

PROVERBS 1:33

Except the Lord build the house, they labour
in vain that build it: except the Lord keep
the city, the watchman waketh but in vain.
It is vain for you to rise up early, to sit up late,
to eat the bread of sorrows: for so he giveth
his beloved sleep.
Lo, children are an heritage of the Lord: and
the fruit of the womb is his reward.
As arrows are in the hand of a mighty man; so
are children of the youth.
Happy is the man that hath his quiver full of
them: they shall not be ashamed, but they
shall speak with the enemies in the gate.

PSALM 127:1–5

But the Lord is faithful, who shall stablish
you, and keep you from evil.

2 THESSALONIANS 3:3

O Lord, thou hast searched me, and known me.

Thou knowest my downsitting and mine
uprising, thou understandest my thought
afar off.

Thou compassest my path and my lying down,
and art acquainted with all my ways.

For there is not a word in my tongue, but, lo,
O Lord, thou knowest it altogether.

Thou hast beset me behind and before, and
laid thine hand upon me.

Such knowledge is too wonderful for me; it is
high, I cannot attain unto it.

Whither shall I go from thy spirit? or whither
shall I flee from thy presence?

If I ascend up into heaven, thou art there: if
I make my bed in hell, behold, thou art
there.

If I take the wings of the morning, and dwell in
the uttermost parts of the sea;

Even there shall thy hand lead me, and thy
right hand shall hold me.

If I say, Surely the darkness shall cover me;
  even the night shall be light about me.
Yea, the darkness hideth not from thee; but the
  night shineth as the day: the darkness and
  the light are both alike to thee.
For thou hast possessed my reins: thou hast
  covered me in my mother's womb.
I will praise thee; for I am fearfully and wonder-
  fully made: marvellous are thy works; and
  that my soul knoweth right well.

PSALM 139:1–14

But know that the LORD hath set apart him
  that is godly for himself: the LORD will
  hear when I call unto him. . . .
Thou hast put gladness in my heart, more than
  in the time that their corn and their wine
  increased.
I will both lay me down in peace, and sleep:
  for thou, LORD, only makest me dwell in
  safety.

PSALM 4:3, 7–8

But now thus saith the LORD that created thee, O Jacob, and he that formed thee, O Israel, Fear not: for I have redeemed thee, I have called thee by thy name; thou art mine.

When thou passest through the waters, I will be with thee; and through the rivers, they shall not overflow thee: when thou walkest through the fire, thou shalt not be burned; neither shall the flame kindle upon thee.

ISAIAH 43:1–2

Stand on His Promises

For God is not unrighteous to forget your work and labour of love, which ye have shewed toward his name, in that ye have ministered to the saints, and do minister.

And we desire that every one of you do shew the same diligence to the full assurance of hope unto the end:

That ye be not slothful, but followers of them who through faith and patience inherit the promises.

Hebrews 6:10–12

Whereby are given unto us exceeding great and precious promises: that by these ye might be partakers of the divine nature, having escaped the corruption that is in the world through lust.

And beside this, giving all diligence, add to your faith virtue; and to virtue knowledge;

And to knowledge temperance; and to temperance patience; and to patience godliness;

And to godliness brotherly kindness; and to brotherly kindness charity.

For if these things be in you, and abound, they make you that ye shall neither be barren nor unfruitful in the knowledge of our Lord Jesus Christ.

2 PETER 1:4–8

The Lord is not slack concerning his promise, as some men count slackness; but is longsuffering to us-ward, not willing that any should perish, but that all should come to repentance.

2 PETER 3:9

And said, If thou wilt diligently hearken to the voice of the LORD thy God, and wilt do that which is right in his sight, and wilt give ear to his commandments, and keep all his statutes, I will put none of these diseases upon thee, which I have brought upon the Egyptians: for I am the LORD that healeth thee.

EXODUS 15:26

For ye are all the children of God by faith in Christ Jesus.

For as many of you as have been baptized into Christ have put on Christ.

There is neither Jew nor Greek, there is neither bond nor free, there is neither male nor female: for ye are all one in Christ Jesus.

And if ye be Christ's, then are ye Abraham's seed, and heirs according to the promise.

GALATIANS 3:26–29

And this is the confidence that we have in him, that, if we ask any thing according to his will, he heareth us:

And if we know that he hear us, whatsoever we ask, we know that we have the petitions that we desired of him.

1 John 5:14–15

Moreover he must have a good report of them which are without; lest he fall into reproach and the snare of the devil.

Likewise must the deacons be grave, not doubletongued, not given to much wine, not greedy of filthy lucre.

1 Timothy 3:7–8

GO HIS WAY

And this I say, lest any man should beguile you with enticing words.

For though I be absent in the flesh, yet am I with you in the spirit, joying and beholding your order, and the stedfastness of your faith in Christ.

As ye have therefore received Christ Jesus the Lord, so walk ye in him:

Rooted and built up in him, and stablished in the faith, as ye have been taught, abounding therein with thanksgiving.

COLOSSIANS 2:4–7

Let love be without dissimulation. Abhor that which is evil; cleave to that which is good.

Be kindly affectioned one to another with brotherly love; in honour preferring one another;

Not slothful in business; fervent in spirit; serving the Lord;

Rejoicing in hope; patient in tribulation; continuing instant in prayer;

Distributing to the necessity of saints; given to hospitality.

Bless them which persecute you: bless, and curse not.

Rejoice with them that do rejoice, and weep with them that weep.

Be of the same mind one toward another. Mind not high things, but condescend to men of low estate. Be not wise in your own conceits.

Recompense to no man evil for evil. Provide things honest in the sight of all men.

If it be possible, as much as lieth in you, live peaceably with all men.

ROMANS 12:9–18

Trust in the LORD with all thine heart; and
lean not unto thine own understanding.
In all thy ways acknowledge him, and he shall
direct thy paths.

PROVERBS 3:5–6

I will bless the LORD, who hath given me
counsel: my reins also instruct me in the
night seasons.
I have set the LORD always before me: because
he is at my right hand, I shall not be
moved.
Therefore my heart is glad, and my glory
rejoiceth: my flesh also shall rest in
hope. . . .
Thou wilt shew me the path of life: in thy
presence is fulness of joy; at thy right hand
there are pleasures for evermore.

PSALM 16:7–9, 11

For I know the thoughts that I think toward
you, saith the LORD, thoughts of peace, and
not of evil, to give you an expected end.
Then shall ye call upon me, and ye shall go and
pray unto me, and I will hearken unto you.
And ye shall seek me, and find me, when ye
shall search for me with all your heart.

JEREMIAH 29:11–13

As for God, his way is perfect: the word of the
LORD is tried: he is a buckler to all those
that trust in him.
For who is God save the LORD? or who is a rock
save our God?
It is God that girdeth me with strength, and
maketh my way perfect.

PSALM 18:30–32

GOD TEACHES A SISTER IN
FAITH HOW TO . . .

BASK IN HIS PRESENCE

~~~•~~~

Rejoice in the LORD, O ye righteous: for praise
 is comely for the upright.

Praise the LORD with harp: sing unto him
 with the psaltery and an instrument of ten
 strings.

Sing unto him a new song; play skilfully with a
 loud noise.

For the word of the LORD is right; and all his
 works are done in truth.

He loveth righteousness and judgment: the
 earth is full of the goodness of the LORD.

PSALM 33:1–5

O God, my heart is fixed; I will sing and give
praise, even with my glory.

Awake, psaltery and harp: I myself will awake
early.

I will praise thee, O LORD, among the people:
and I will sing praises unto thee among the
nations.

For thy mercy is great above the heavens: and
thy truth reacheth unto the clouds.

Be thou exalted, O God, above the heavens:
and thy glory above all the earth;

That thy beloved may be delivered: save with
thy right hand, and answer me.

PSALM 108:1–6

O God, thou art terrible out of thy holy places:
the God of Israel is he that giveth strength
and power unto his people. Blessed be
God.

PSALM 68:35

When I remember thee upon my bed, and
meditate on thee in the night watches.
Because thou hast been my help, therefore in
the shadow of thy wings will I rejoice.
My soul followeth hard after thee: thy right
hand upholdeth me.

PSALM 63:6–8

I have set the LORD always before me: because
he is at my right hand, I shall not be
moved.
Therefore my heart is glad, and my glory
rejoiceth: my flesh also shall rest in hope.
For thou wilt not leave my soul in hell; neither
wilt thou suffer thine Holy One to see
corruption.
Thou wilt shew me the path of life: in thy
presence is fulness of joy; at thy right hand
there are pleasures for evermore.

PSALM 16:8–11

Ye that love the LORD, hate evil: he preserveth
the souls of his saints; he delivereth them
out of the hand of the wicked.
Light is sown for the righteous, and gladness
for the upright in heart.
Rejoice in the LORD, ye righteous; and give
thanks at the remembrance of his holiness.

PSALM 97:10–12

STAND IN THE GAP

And Moses cried unto the LORD, saying,
Heal her now, O God, I beseech thee.

NUMBERS 12:13

Family is a very complex unit of personalities. Those personalities can bring us overwhelming joy, as well as pain and disappointment. Disagreements aren't unusual between family members and can lead to damaging grudges. These situations can handicap the ability of the family to function in love and harmony because no one is willing to bury the hatchet.

Moses' siblings, Aaron and Miriam, spoke against Moses and his leadership because he married an Ethiopian woman, Zipporah. God did not take this lightly! Moses, Aaron, and Miriam got called into a meeting. In this meeting, God spoke for Moses because he was an upright man. As a punishment, Miriam was struck with leprosy, which could have been the end of her story.

Even though Moses was in the right, he chose to stand in the gap and plead to the Lord for his sister. Because of his love for her, he was willing to forgive Miriam's sin against him and his wife. God heard Moses' prayer and Miriam was cleansed. Moses' act of love is a testament to his character and gives us insight into his close relationship with God.

～ PRACTICAL APPLICATION ～

If you choose to be an active part of your family, you may face many moments similar to the one Moses faced. When family hurts you, you will come to a crossroad. Will you choose to hold on to the anger, or will you react as Moses did?

You are a strong woman, and God is working in your life. He will stand by you as you choose to walk in love and forgive the offenses of your family. It's not easy, but as you ask God's help in this, he will give you the strength you need. Release the family members who have hurt and offended you. Pray for them, and watch as God continues to show you his favor.

～⁓ PRAYER ⁓～

Father, I come before you with a wounded heart. Please fill my heart with love and forgiveness toward those who have hurt me. I pray for mercy, and I stand in the gap, asking that you will touch their lives as you reveal yourself to them.

—Joann Rosario Condrey

TRULY LOVE OTHERS

Let brotherly love continue.

Be not forgetful to entertain strangers: for thereby some have entertained angels unawares. . . .

Let your conversation be without covetousness; and be content with such things as ye have: for he hath said, I will never leave thee, nor forsake thee.

HEBREWS 13:1–2, 5

This is my commandment, That ye love one another, as I have loved you.

Greater love hath no man than this, that a man lay down his life for his friends.

JOHN 15:12–13

For our comely parts have no need: but God hath tempered the body together, having given more abundant honour to that part which lacked.

That there should be no schism in the body; but that the members should have the same care one for another.

And whether one member suffer, all the members suffer with it; or one member be honoured, all the members rejoice with it.

1 Corinthians 12:24–26

For, brethren, ye have been called unto liberty; only use not liberty for an occasion to the flesh, but by love serve one another.

Galatians 5:13

Let all your things be done with charity.

1 Corinthians 16:14

Two are better than one; because they have a good reward for their labour.

For if they fall, the one will lift up his fellow: but woe to him that is alone when he falleth; for he hath not another to help him up.

Again, if two lie together, then they have heat: but how can one be warm alone?

ECCLESIASTES 4:9–11

As thou knowest not what is the way of the spirit, nor how the bones do grow in the womb of her that is with child: even so thou knowest not the works of God who maketh all.

In the morning sow thy seed, and in the evening withhold not thine hand: for thou knowest not whether shall prosper, either this or that, or whether they both shall be alike good.

ECCLESIASTES 11:5–6

BE A DOER OF GOOD

~·~·~

For he that soweth to his flesh shall of the flesh reap corruption; but he that soweth to the Spirit shall of the Spirit reap life everlasting.

And let us not be weary in well doing: for in due season we shall reap, if we faint not.

GALATIANS 6:8–9

Give, and it shall be given unto you; good measure, pressed down, and shaken together, and running over, shall men give into your bosom. For with the same measure that ye mete withal it shall be measured to you again.

LUKE 6:38

Defend the poor and fatherless: do justice to
the afflicted and needy.
Deliver the poor and needy: rid them out of the
hand of the wicked.

Psalm 82:3–4

Hereby perceive we the love of God, because
he laid down his life for us: and we ought to lay
down our lives for the brethren.

But whoso hath this world's good, and seeth
his brother have need, and shutteth up his bowels
of compassion from him, how dwelleth the love
of God in him?

My little children, let us not love in word,
neither in tongue; but in deed and in truth.

1 John 3:16–18

She stretcheth out her hand to the poor; yea, she
reacheth forth her hands to the needy.

Proverbs 31:20

He that receiveth you receiveth me, and he that receiveth me receiveth him that sent me.

He that receiveth a prophet in the name of a prophet shall receive a prophet's reward; and he that receiveth a righteous man in the name of a righteous man shall receive a righteous man's reward.

And whosoever shall give to drink unto one of these little ones a cup of cold water only in the name of a disciple, verily I say unto you, he shall in no wise lose his reward.

MATTHEW 10:40–42

Finally, be ye all of one mind, having compassion one of another, love as brethren, be pitiful, be courteous:

Not rendering evil for evil, or railing for railing: but contrariwise blessing; knowing that ye are thereunto called, that ye should inherit a blessing.

1 PETER 3:8–9

SERVE OTHERS

But it shall not be so among you: but whosoever will be great among you, let him be your minister;

And whosoever will be chief among you, let him be your servant:

Even as the Son of man came not to be ministered unto, but to minister, and to give his life a ransom for many.

MATTHEW 20:26–28

For, brethren, ye have been called unto liberty; only use not liberty for an occasion to the flesh, but by love serve one another.

GALATIANS 5:13

As every man hath received the gift, even so minister the same one to another, as good stewards of the manifold grace of God.

If any man speak, let him speak as the oracles of God; if any man minister, let him do it as of the ability which God giveth: that God in all things may be glorified through Jesus Christ, to whom be praise and dominion for ever and ever. Amen.

1 Peter 4:10–11

Defend the poor and fatherless: do justice to
the afflicted and needy.
Deliver the poor and needy: rid them out of the
hand of the wicked.
They know not, neither will they understand;
they walk on in darkness: all the foundations of the earth are out of course.

Psalm 82:3–5

And whatsoever ye do, do it heartily, as to the Lord, and not unto men;

Knowing that of the Lord ye shall receive the reward of the inheritance: for ye serve the Lord Christ.

Colossians 3:23–24

But Jesus called them to him, and saith unto them, Ye know that they which are accounted to rule over the Gentiles exercise lordship over them; and their great ones exercise authority upon them.

But so shall it not be among you: but whosoever will be great among you, shall be your minister:

And whosoever of you will be the chiefest, shall be servant of all.

For even the Son of man came not to be ministered unto, but to minister, and to give his life a ransom for many.

Mark 10:42–45

He that is faithful in that which is least is faithful also in much: and he that is unjust in the least is unjust also in much.

If therefore ye have not been faithful in the unrighteous mammon, who will commit to your trust the true riches?

And if ye have not been faithful in that which is another man's, who shall give you that which is your own?

No servant can serve two masters: for either he will hate the one, and love the other; or else he will hold to the one, and despise the other. Ye cannot serve God and mammon.

LUKE 16:10–13

PRAY FOR OTHERS

Give ear, O LORD, unto my prayer; and attend
   to the voice of my supplications.
In the day of my trouble I will call upon thee:
   for thou wilt answer me. . . .
Teach me thy way, O LORD; I will walk in thy
   truth: unite my heart to fear thy name.
I will praise thee, O Lord my God, with all
   my heart: and I will glorify thy name for
   evermore.
For great is thy mercy toward me: and thou
   hast delivered my soul from the lowest hell.

PSALM 86:6–7, 11–13

Call unto me, and I will answer thee, and show thee great and mighty things, which thou knowest not.

JEREMIAH 33:3

And take the helmet of salvation, and the sword of the Spirit, which is the word of God:

Praying always with all prayer and supplication in the Spirit, and watching thereunto with all perseverance and supplication for all saints.

EPHESIANS 6:17–18

And this is the confidence that we have in him, that, if we ask any thing according to his will, he heareth us:

And if we know that he hear us, whatsoever we ask, we know that we have the petitions that we desired of him.

1 JOHN 5:14–15

Confess your faults one to another, and pray one for another, that ye may be healed. The effectual fervent prayer of a righteous man availeth much.

JAMES 5:16

Come and hear, all ye that fear God, and I will
    declare what he hath done for my soul.
I cried unto him with my mouth, and he was
    extolled with my tongue.
If I regard iniquity in my heart, the Lord will
    not hear me:
But verily God hath heard me; he hath
    attended to the voice of my prayer.
Blessed be God, which hath not turned away
    my prayer, nor his mercy from me.

PSALM 66:16–20

Sing unto God, sing praises to his name: extol
him that rideth upon the heavens by his
name JAH, and rejoice before him.
A father of the fatherless, and a judge of the
widows, is God in his holy habitation.
God setteth the solitary in families: he
bringeth out those which are bound with
chains: but the rebellious dwell in a dry
land.

PSALM 68:4–6

Give ear to my words, O LORD, consider my
meditation.
Hearken unto the voice of my cry, my King,
and my God: for unto thee will I pray.
My voice shalt thou hear in the morning, O
LORD; in the morning will I direct my
prayer unto thee, and will look up.

PSALM 5:1–3

I will praise thee, O LORD, with my whole
heart; I will shew forth all thy marvellous
works.
I will be glad and rejoice in thee: I will sing
praise to thy name, O thou most High.
When mine enemies are turned back, they
shall fall and perish at thy presence. . . .
The LORD also will be a refuge for the
oppressed, a refuge in times of trouble.
And they that know thy name will put their
trust in thee: for thou, LORD, hast not
forsaken them that seek thee.

PSALM 9:1–3, 9–10

HAVE THE JOY OF THE LORD

~ • ~ • ~

I will praise thee with my whole heart: before
    the gods will I sing praise unto thee.
I will worship toward thy holy temple, and
    praise thy name for thy lovingkindness and
    for thy truth: for thou hast magnified thy
    word above all thy name.
In the day when I cried thou answeredst me,
    and strengthenedst me with strength in my
    soul.

PSALM 138:1–3

Now the God of hope fill you with all joy and
peace in believing, that ye may abound in hope,
through the power of the Holy Ghost.

ROMANS 15:13

O LORD, how manifold are thy works! in
   wisdom hast thou made them all: the earth
   is full of thy riches.
So is this great and wide sea, wherein are
   things creeping innumerable, both small
   and great beasts.
There go the ships: there is that leviathan,
   whom thou hast made to play therein.
These wait all upon thee; that thou mayest give
   them their meat in due season.
That thou givest them they gather: thou
   openest thine hand, they are filled with
   good. . . .
I will sing unto the LORD as long as I live: I
   will sing praise to my God while I have my
   being.
My meditation of him shall be sweet: I will be
   glad in the LORD.

PSALM 104:24–28, 33–34

O give thanks unto the LORD; call upon his name:
make known his deeds among the people.
Sing unto him, sing psalms unto him: talk ye
of all his wondrous works.
Glory ye in his holy name: let the heart of them
rejoice that seek the LORD.
Seek the LORD, and his strength: seek his face
evermore.
Remember his marvellous works that he hath
done; his wonders, and the judgments of
his mouth.

PSALM 105:1–5

As the Father hath loved me, so have I loved
you: continue ye in my love.

If ye keep my commandments, ye shall abide
in my love; even as I have kept my Father's commandments, and abide in his love.

These things have I spoken unto you, that
my joy might remain in you, and that your joy
might be full.

JOHN 15:9–11

Sing unto the Lord, O ye saints of his, and give
thanks at the remembrance of his holiness.
For his anger endureth but a moment; in his
favour is life: weeping may endure for a
night, but joy cometh in the morning.

PSALM 30:4–5

The Lord thy God in the midst of thee is mighty; he will save, he will rejoice over thee with joy; he will rest in his love, he will joy over thee with singing.

ZEPHANIAH 3:17

Great is the Lord, and greatly to be praised;
and his greatness is unsearchable.
One generation shall praise thy works to
another, and shall declare thy mighty acts.
I will speak of the glorious honour of thy
majesty, and of thy wondrous works.

PSALM 145:3–5

GOD CROWNS A
SISTER IN FAITH
WITH . . .

HIS WISDOM

The queen of Sheba, the wealthy and powerful sovereign of a southern nation,
heard of King Solomon's wisdom. She trav-
eled to Jerusalem to meet with him and ask
him some difficult questions. She was accom-
panied by a large group of attendants and by
camels carrying spices, jewels, and a large
amount of gold as a gift for the king—her
great wealth on display for all to see.

When they met, the queen of Sheba asked Solomon a multitude of questions, and he answered them all. The queen was amazed by Solomon's kingdom and by his wisdom, riches, and relationship with God. She was struck by the happiness his subjects enjoyed. Before she left, she showered Solomon with all the gifts she had brought; Solomon reciprocated with lavish gifts for the powerful queen.

The queen's trip was a success. Not only did she return home with many gifts, but she also received the lasting benefit of Solomon's godly wisdom (see 1 Kings 10:1–14; 2 Chronicles 9:1–12; Matthew 12:42).

The queen of Sheba gave us this to remember: when we humble ourselves on the quest for wisdom, the riches gained will be worth far more than the price of our pride.

—Keren Heath

GREAT WORTH

～·～·～

Who can find a virtuous woman? for her price
is far above rubies.

PROVERBS 31:10

She openeth her mouth with wisdom; and in
her tongue is the law of kindness.
She looketh well to the ways of her household,
and eateth not the bread of idleness.
Her children arise up, and call her blessed; her
husband also, and he praiseth her.

PROVERBS 31:26–28

The hoary head is a crown of glory, if it be
found in the way of righteousness.

Proverbs 16:31

Favour is deceitful, and beauty is vain: but a
woman that feareth the Lord, she shall be
praised.
Give her of the fruit of her hands; and let her
own works praise her in the gates.

Proverbs 31:30–31

Every wise woman buildeth her house: but the
foolish plucketh it down with her hands.

Proverbs 14:1

The heart of her husband doth safely trust in
her, so that he shall have no need of spoil.
She will do him good and not evil all the days
of her life.

Proverbs 31:11–12

She considereth a field, and buyeth it: with the
fruit of her hands she planteth a vineyard.

PROVERBS 31:16

A virtuous woman is a crown to her husband:
but she that maketh ashamed is as
rottenness in his bones.

PROVERBS 12:4

And this I pray, that your love may abound
yet more and more in knowledge and in all
judgment;

That ye may approve things that are excellent; that ye may be sincere and without offence
till the day of Christ.

PHILIPPIANS 1:9–10

GOD CROWNS A SISTER IN
FAITH WITH . . .

MUCH FRUIT

The Lord by wisdom hath founded the earth;
    by understanding hath he established the
    heavens.
By his knowledge the depths are broken up,
    and the clouds drop down the dew.

PROVERBS 3:19–20

Wisdom crieth without; she uttereth her voice
    in the streets:
She crieth in the chief place of concourse, in
    the openings of the gates: in the city she
    uttereth her words.

PROVERBS 1:20–21

I am the vine, ye are the branches: He that abideth in me, and I in him, the same bringeth forth much fruit: for without me ye can do nothing. . . .

Ye have not chosen me, but I have chosen you, and ordained you, that ye should go and bring forth fruit, and that your fruit should remain: that whatsoever ye shall ask of the Father in my name, he may give it you.

JOHN 15:5, 16

I will instruct thee and teach thee in the way
    which thou shalt go: I will guide thee with
    mine eye.

PSALM 32:8

And the LORD shall guide thee continually, and satisfy thy soul in drought, and make fat thy bones: and thou shalt be like a watered garden, and like a spring of water, whose waters fail not.

ISAIAH 58:11

The LORD possessed me in the beginning of his
way, before his works of old.

I was set up from everlasting, from the
beginning, or ever the earth was.

When there were no depths, I was brought
forth; when there were no fountains
abounding with water.

Before the mountains were settled, before the
hills was I brought forth:

While as yet he had not made the earth, nor
the fields, nor the highest part of the dust
of the world.

When he prepared the heavens, I was there:
when he set a compass upon the face of the
depth:

When he established the clouds above: when he
strengthened the fountains of the deep:

When he gave to the sea his decree, that the
waters should not pass his commandment:
when he appointed the foundations of the
earth:

Then I was by him, as one brought up with
    him: and I was daily his delight, rejoicing
    always before him;
Rejoicing in the habitable part of his earth; and
    my delights were with the sons of men.

PROVERBS 8:22–31

[God] only is my rock and my salvation: he is
    my defence; I shall not be moved.
In God is my salvation and my glory: the rock
    of my strength, and my refuge, is in God.

PSALM 62:6–7

A Righteous Reputation

I wisdom dwell with prudence, and find out
knowledge of witty inventions.
The fear of the Lord is to hate evil: pride,
and arrogancy, and the evil way, and the
froward mouth, do I hate.
Counsel is mine, and sound wisdom: I am
understanding; I have strength.

PROVERBS 8:12–14

The words of a man's mouth are as deep
waters, and the wellspring of wisdom as a
flowing brook.

PROVERBS 18:4

Now therefore hearken unto me, O ye children:
for blessed are they that keep my ways.
Hear instruction, and be wise, and refuse it
not.
Blessed is the man that heareth me, watching
daily at my gates, waiting at the posts of
my doors.
For whoso findeth me findeth life, and shall
obtain favour of the LORD.
But he that sinneth against me wrongeth his
own soul: all they that hate me love death.

PROVERBS 8:32–36

What man is he that feareth the LORD? him
shall he teach in the way that he shall
choose.
His soul shall dwell at ease; and his seed shall
inherit the earth.

PSALM 25:12–13

He that getteth wisdom loveth his own soul:
he that keepeth understanding shall find
good.

PROVERBS 19:8

Hear, O my son, and receive my sayings; and
the years of thy life shall be many.
I have taught thee in the way of wisdom; I have
led thee in right paths.
When thou goest, thy steps shall not be
straitened; and when thou runnest, thou
shalt not stumble.
Take fast hold of instruction; let her not go:
keep her; for she is thy life.

PROVERBS 4:10–13

A virtuous woman is a crown to her husband.

PROVERBS 12:4

GOD CROWNS A SISTER IN
FAITH WITH . . .

A PURE HEART

A foolish woman is clamorous: she is simple,
and knoweth nothing.
For she sitteth at the door of her house, on a
seat in the high places of the city,
To call passengers who go right on their ways:
Whoso is simple, let him turn in hither: and as
for him that wanteth understanding, she
saith to him,
Stolen waters are sweet, and bread eaten in
secret is pleasant.
But he knoweth not that the dead are there;
and that her guests are in the depths of
hell.

PROVERBS 9:13–18

Say unto wisdom, Thou art my sister; and call
    understanding thy kinswoman.

PROVERBS 7:4

The fear of the LORD tendeth to life: and he
    that hath it shall abide satisfied; he shall
    not be visited with evil.

PROVERBS 19:23

A gracious woman retaineth honour: and
    strong men retain riches.

PROVERBS 11:16

Favour is deceitful, and beauty is vain: but a
    woman that feareth the LORD, she shall be
    praised.

PROVERBS 31:30

She stretcheth out her hand to the poor; yea,
    she reacheth forth her hands to the needy.

PROVERBS 31:20

When wisdom entereth into thine heart, and
knowledge is pleasant unto thy soul;
Discretion shall preserve thee, understanding
shall keep thee:
To deliver thee from the way of the evil man,
from the man that speaketh froward
things;
Who leave the paths of uprightness, to walk in
the ways of darkness;
Who rejoice to do evil, and delight in the
frowardness of the wicked;
Whose ways are crooked, and they froward in
their paths. . . .
That thou mayest walk in the way of good men,
and keep the paths of the righteous.
For the upright shall dwell in the land, and the
perfect shall remain in it.
But the wicked shall be cut off from the earth,
and the transgressors shall be rooted out
of it.

PROVERBS 2:10–15, 20–22

A Sanctified Marriage

~~~

The heart of her husband doth safely trust in
    her, so that he shall have no need of spoil.
She will do him good and not evil all the days
    of her life.

<div align="right">PROVERBS 31:11–12</div>

Wives, submit yourselves unto your own
husbands, as unto the Lord.

For the husband is the head of the wife, even
as Christ is the head of the church: and he is the
saviour of the body.

Therefore as the church is subject unto
Christ, so let the wives be to their own husbands
in every thing.

<div align="right">EPHESIANS 5:22–24</div>

Nevertheless let every one of you in particular so love his wife even as himself; and the wife see that she reverence her husband.

EPHESIANS 5:33

Her husband is known in the gates, when he sitteth among the elders of the land.

PROVERBS 31:23

Likewise, ye wives, be in subjection to your own husbands; that, if any obey not the word, they also may without the word be won by the conversation of the wives.

1 PETER 3:1

The aged women likewise, that they be in behaviour as becometh holiness, not false accusers, not given to much wine, teachers of good things;

That they may teach the young women to be sober, to love their husbands, to love their children.

TITUS 2:3–4

ABIDING FAITH

But ye, beloved, building up yourselves on your most holy faith, praying in the Holy Ghost,

Keep yourselves in the love of God, looking for the mercy of our Lord Jesus Christ unto eternal life.

JUDE VV. 20–21

It is a good thing to give thanks unto the LORD,
   and to sing praises unto thy name, O Most
   High:
To shew forth thy lovingkindness in the
   morning, and thy faithfulness every night.

PSALM 92:1–2

Blessed is the people that know the joyful
     sound: they shall walk, O LORD, in the
     light of thy countenance.
In thy name shall they rejoice all the day: and
     in thy righteousness shall they be exalted.
For thou art the glory of their strength: and in
     thy favour our horn shall be exalted.

PSALM 89:15–17

But the fruit of the Spirit is love, joy, peace,
longsuffering, gentleness, goodness, faith,
     Meekness, temperance: against such there is
no law.

GALATIANS 5:22–23

Who is a wise man and endued with
knowledge among you? let him shew out of a
good conversation his works with meekness of
wisdom.

JAMES 3:13

I will sing of the mercies of the LORD for ever:
with my mouth will I make known thy
faithfulness to all generations.
For I have said, Mercy shall be built up for
ever: thy faithfulness shalt thou establish
in the very heavens.

PSALM 89:1–2

For ever, O LORD, thy word is settled in heaven.
Thy faithfulness is unto all generations: thou
hast established the earth, and it abideth.
They continue this day according to thine
ordinances: for all are thy servants.

PSALM 119:89–91

O love the LORD, all ye his saints: for the LORD
preserveth the faithful, and plentifully
rewardeth the proud doer.

PSALM 31:23

ONENESS WITH HER HUSBAND

Many daughters have done virtuously, but thou
excellest them all.

PROVERBS 31:29

Finally, brethren, whatsoever things are true,
whatsoever things are honest, whatsoever things
are just, whatsoever things are pure, whatsoever
things are lovely, whatsoever things are of good
report; if there be any virtue, and if there be any
praise, think on these things.

PHILIPPIANS 4:8

She openeth her mouth with wisdom; and in
her tongue is the law of kindness.

PROVERBS 31:26

Therefore shall a man leave his father and his mother, and shall cleave unto his wife: and they shall be one flesh.

Genesis 2:24

The righteousness of the upright shall deliver them: but transgressors shall be taken in their own naughtiness.

Proverbs 11:6

The thoughts of the wicked are an abomination to the Lord: but the words of the pure are pleasant words.

Proverbs 15:26

Therefore as the church is subject unto Christ, so let the wives be to their own husbands in every thing.

Ephesians 5:24

Blessed are the pure in heart: for they shall see God.

Matthew 5:8

GOD DELIGHTS IN A SISTER IN FAITH WHO . . .

KEEPS IT REAL

Take heed to yourselves: If thy brother trespass against thee, rebuke him; and if he repent, forgive him.

LUKE 17:3

It's virtually impossible to receive direction or reproof from relationships on social media outlets like Facebook, LinkedIn, and Twitter. No matter how inspired we are after reading a post or a message, there's nothing like meeting one-on-one over a cup of coffee with a girlfriend to get us back on track. We all need one or two trusted friends who just keep it real with us. They share the victories we experience at home, at work, and in the community and our disappointments when we fail.

When Jesus set his face to Jerusalem, the Scriptures record that he sent his followers out two by two. Because he knew the triumphs and adversities they would face, he wanted them to have each other's backs when times got tough. That same accountability can be present today in the context of a healthy, safe Christian community. And although we live extremely busy lives, seeking Christian accountability is one of the wisest things we can do to safeguard our souls.

～ PRACTICAL APPLICATION ～

Accountability simply means being answerable. As believers in Christ, we are accountable to God first (Romans 14:11–12) and then to one another (1 Corinthians 12:20–21, 26). The process of finding an accountability partner begins with prayer. First, ask God to send us someone to be accountable to. Second, identify those women and ask them to pray about joining with us. Finally, take the risk to be real! Note: our flesh nature will buck against the idea of someone else being able to question our choices or behavior, but it is through these kinds of real relationships that we become spiritually mature.

~⌣ PRAYER ⌣~

Heavenly Father, would you help me find a sister in faith to be accountable to? I pray, even now, that our relationship will be mutually beneficial and totally devoted to your good purposes. Thank you for meeting all my needs according to your riches in glory. Amen.

—Lakeba Williams

SEEKS HIS FACE

One thing have I desired of the LORD, that
    will I seek after; that I may dwell in the
    house of the LORD all the days of my life,
    to behold the beauty of the LORD, and to
    enquire in his temple.
For in the time of trouble he shall hide me in
    his pavilion: in the secret of his tabernacle
    shall he hide me; he shall set me up upon
    a rock.

PSALM 27:4–5

Delight thyself also in the LORD: and he shall
    give thee the desires of thine heart.
Commit thy way unto the LORD; trust also in
    him; and he shall bring it to pass.

PSALM 37:4–5

I love them that love me; and those that seek
me early shall find me.

PROVERBS 8:17

Seek ye the LORD while he may be found, call
ye upon him while he is near:
Let the wicked forsake his way, and the
unrighteous man his thoughts: and let him
return unto the LORD, and he will have
mercy upon him; and to our God, for he
will abundantly pardon.

ISAIAH 55:6–7

For I know the thoughts that I think toward you,
saith the LORD, thoughts of peace, and not of
evil, to give you an expected end.
Then shall ye call upon me, and ye shall go and
pray unto me, and I will hearken unto you.
And ye shall seek me, and find me, when ye
shall search for me with all your heart.

JEREMIAH 29:11–13

Seek the LORD, and his strength: seek his face evermore.

PSALM 105:4

Ask, and it shall be given you; seek, and ye shall find; knock, and it shall be opened unto you:

For every one that asketh receiveth; and he that seeketh findeth; and to him that knocketh it shall be opened.

MATTHEW 7:7–8

Is His True Friend

Be not afraid of sudden fear, neither of the
desolation of the wicked, when it cometh.
For the Lord shall be thy confidence, and shall
keep thy foot from being taken.

PROVERBS 3:25–26

But the Lord is faithful, who shall stablish
you, and keep you from evil.

And we have confidence in the Lord touch-
ing you, that ye both do and will do the things
which we command you.

And the Lord direct your hearts into the love
of God, and into the patient waiting for Christ.

2 THESSALONIANS 3:3–5

Grace and peace be multiplied unto you through the knowledge of God, and of Jesus our Lord,

According as his divine power hath given unto us all things that pertain unto life and godliness, through the knowledge of him that hath called us to glory and virtue:

Whereby are given unto us exceeding great and precious promises: that by these ye might be partakers of the divine nature, having escaped the corruption that is in the world through lust.

2 Peter 1:2–4

Cast not away therefore your confidence, which hath great recompence of reward.

For ye have need of patience, that, after ye have done the will of God, ye might receive the promise.

Hebrews 10:35–36

And this is the confidence that we have in him, that, if we ask any thing according to his will, he heareth us:

And if we know that he hear us, whatsoever we ask, we know that we have the petitions that we desired of him.

1 John 5:14–15

I have fought a good fight, I have finished my course, I have kept the faith:

Henceforth there is laid up for me a crown of righteousness, which the Lord, the righteous judge, shall give me at that day: and not to me only, but unto all them also that love his appearing.

2 Timothy 4:7–8

Christ as a son over his own house; whose house are we, if we hold fast the confidence and the rejoicing of the hope firm unto the end.

Hebrews 3:6

In thee, O LORD, do I put my trust: let me
    never be put to confusion.
Deliver me in thy righteousness, and cause me
    to escape: incline thine ear unto me, and
    save me. . . .
For thou art my hope, O Lord GOD: thou art
    my trust from my youth.

PSALM 71:1–2, 5

Is in Christ Jesus

There is therefore now no condemnation to them which are in Christ Jesus, who walk not after the flesh, but after the Spirit.

For the law of the Spirit of life in Christ Jesus hath made me free from the law of sin and death.

ROMANS 8:1–2

In whom we have redemption through his blood, the forgiveness of sins, according to the riches of his grace;

Wherein he hath abounded toward us in all wisdom and prudence.

EPHESIANS 1:7–8

If we say that we have no sin, we deceive ourselves, and the truth is not in us.

If we confess our sins, he is faithful and just to forgive us our sins, and to cleanse us from all unrighteousness.

1 John 1:8–9

For as the heaven is high above the earth, so
    great is his mercy toward them that fear
    him.
As far as the east is from the west, so far hath
    he removed our transgressions from us.

Psalm 103:11–12

If my people, which are called by my name, shall humble themselves, and pray, and seek my face, and turn from their wicked ways; then will I hear from heaven, and will forgive their sin, and will heal their land.

2 Chronicles 7:14

In whom also ye are circumcised with the circumcision made without hands, in putting off the body of the sins of the flesh by the circumcision of Christ . . .

And you, being dead in your sins and the uncircumcision of your flesh, hath he quickened together with him, having forgiven you all trespasses;

Blotting out the handwriting of ordinances that was against us, which was contrary to us, and took it out of the way, nailing it to his cross.

Colossians 2:11, 13–14

Who hath delivered us from the power of darkness, and hath translated us into the kingdom of his dear Son:

In whom we have redemption through his blood, even the forgiveness of sins.

Colossians 1:13–14

Now unto him that is able to keep you from falling, and to present you faultless before the presence of his glory with exceeding joy,

To the only wise God our Saviour, be glory and majesty, dominion and power, both now and ever. Amen.

JUDE VV. 24–25

GOD DELIGHTS IN A SISTER
IN FAITH WHO . . .

Is Teachable in His Ways

~·~

Wherefore lay apart all filthiness and super-fluity of naughtiness, and receive with meekness the engrafted word, which is able to save your souls.

But be ye doers of the word, and not hearers only, deceiving your own selves.

JAMES 1:21–22

That we henceforth be no more children, tossed to and fro, and carried about with every wind of doctrine, by the sleight of men, and cunning craftiness, whereby they lie in wait to deceive;

But speaking the truth in love, may grow up into him in all things, which is the head, even Christ.

EPHESIANS 4:14–15

O God, thou art my God; early will I seek thee:
my soul thirsteth for thee, my flesh longeth
for thee in a dry and thirsty land, where no
water is;
To see thy power and thy glory, so as I have
seen thee in the sanctuary.
Because thy lovingkindness is better than life,
my lips shall praise thee.
Thus will I bless thee while I live: I will lift up
my hands in thy name.
My soul shall be satisfied as with marrow and
fatness; and my mouth shall praise thee
with joyful lips:
When I remember thee upon my bed, and
meditate on thee in the night watches.
Because thou hast been my help, therefore in
the shadow of thy wings will I rejoice.
My soul followeth hard after thee: thy right
hand upholdeth me.

PSALM 63:1–8

Abide in me, and I in you. As the branch cannot bear fruit of itself, except it abide in the vine; no more can ye, except ye abide in me.

I am the vine, ye are the branches: He that abideth in me, and I in him, the same bringeth forth much fruit: for without me ye can do nothing. . . .

If ye abide in me, and my words abide in you, ye shall ask what ye will, and it shall be done unto you.

JOHN 15:4–5, 7

This book of the law shall not depart out of thy mouth; but thou shalt meditate therein day and night, that thou mayest observe to do according to all that is written therein: for then thou shalt make thy way prosperous, and then thou shalt have good success.

JOSHUA 1:8

I will instruct thee and teach thee in the way
which thou shalt go: I will guide thee with
mine eye.

PSALM 32:8

Ye therefore, beloved, seeing ye know these things before, beware lest ye also, being led away with the error of the wicked, fall from your own stedfastness.

But grow in grace, and in the knowledge of our Lord and Saviour Jesus Christ. To him be glory both now and for ever. Amen.

2 PETER 3:17–18

TELLS ABOUT HIS GOODNESS

~~~~~ • ~~~~~

What doth it profit, my brethren, though a man say he hath faith, and have not works? can faith save him?

If a brother or sister be naked, and destitute of daily food,

And one of you say unto them, Depart in peace, be ye warmed and filled; notwithstanding ye give them not those things which are needful to the body; what doth it profit?

Even so faith, if it hath not works, is dead, being alone.

JAMES 2:14–17

This is he that came by water and blood, even Jesus Christ; not by water only, but by water and blood. And it is the Spirit that beareth witness, because the Spirit is truth.

For there are three that bear record in heaven, the Father, the Word, and the Holy Ghost: and these three are one.

And there are three that bear witness in earth, the Spirit, and the water, and the blood: and these three agree in one.

If we receive the witness of men, the witness of God is greater: for this is the witness of God which he hath testified of his Son.

He that believeth on the Son of God hath the witness in himself: he that believeth not God hath made him a liar; because he believeth not the record that God gave of his Son.

1 JOHN 5:6–10

[Jesus] did no sin, neither was guile found in his mouth:

Who, when he was reviled, reviled not again; when he suffered, he threatened not; but committed himself to him that judgeth righteously.

1 Peter 2:22–23

Blessed are the undefiled in the way, who walk
    in the law of the Lord.
Blessed are they that keep his testimonies, and
    that seek him with the whole heart.

Psalm 119:1–2

Hereby know we that we dwell in him, and he in us, because he hath given us of his Spirit.

And we have seen and do testify that the Father sent the Son to be the Saviour of the world.

Whosoever shall confess that Jesus is the Son of God, God dwelleth in him, and he in God.

1 John 4:13 15

Quicken me after thy lovingkindness; so shall I
keep the testimony of thy mouth.

Psalm 119:88

Teach me, O Lord, the way of thy statutes; and
I shall keep it unto the end.
Give me understanding, and I shall keep thy
law; yea, I shall observe it with my whole
heart.
Make me to go in the path of thy
commandments; for therein do I delight.
Incline my heart unto thy testimonies, and not
to covetousness.
Turn away mine eyes from beholding vanity;
and quicken thou me in thy way.
Stablish thy word unto thy servant, who is
devoted to thy fear.
Turn away my reproach which I fear: for thy
judgments are good.
Behold, I have longed after thy precepts:
quicken me in thy righteousness.

Psalm 119:33–40

**GOD GIVES
A SISTER IN
FAITH . . .**

STRENGTH

*Iron sharpeneth iron; so a man sharpeneth
the countenance of his friend.*

PROVERBS 27:17

I always thought myself strong. Even as a
child, I had a strong will. Somehow, I grew
up believing that my strength was enough
for me—as long as I was strong, I would be
successful.

As a young married woman, through the Word of God, the challenge of living a Christian life, and interacting with people taught me that my strength is not enough. In order to grow, I need the challenge of strong women connecting with me and holding me accountable for my actions. My mother, my grandmother, my aunts, my mother-in-law, and certain women in the church and community are all available to me. Though not perfect, these women have a strong faith, and they are willing to walk with me through it all.

～ PRACTICAL APPLICATION ～

When "iron sharpeneth iron," it causes friction. And when friction happens, things heat up. We are taught as youngsters to avoid differences. We may come to believe that a person is not our friend unless she always agrees with us. But it is important that we always be willing to exchange ideas and to challenge one another in order to grow.

When we are in the workplace, it is often difficult to have an "iron sharpeneth iron" relationship with coworkers. We often don't trust each other enough to share ideas, fearing that someone will take credit from us or that we will be criticized. But when we share ideas and provoke one another to good works, we become valuable employees, our thoughts become sharper, and we, in turn, can sharpen others. Then the workplace becomes energized and exciting.

Trust the word of the Lord in your workplace today.

~~ PRAYER ~~

Father God, help me be the kind of woman who can challenge other Christian women to be the very best they can be. Father, thank you for the godly women you have given me as examples. Let me be a sharpening tool for others as I look to be sharpened by them as well. In the name of Jesus, I pray. Amen.

—Jamell Meeks

POWER FOR THE JOURNEY

～·～

Shew me thy ways, O Lord; teach me thy
    paths.
Lead me in thy truth, and teach me: for thou
    art the God of my salvation; on thee do I
    wait all the day. . . .
O keep my soul, and deliver me: let me not be
    ashamed; for I put my trust in thee.
Let integrity and uprightness preserve me; for I
    wait on thee.

PSALM 25:4–5, 20–21

The wise in heart will receive commandments:
    but a prating fool shall fall.
He that walketh uprightly walketh surely: but he
    that perverteth his ways shall be known.

PROVERBS 10:8–9

Blessed is the man that walketh not in the
counsel of the ungodly, nor standeth in the
way of sinners, nor sitteth in the seat of the
scornful.

But his delight is in the law of the LORD; and in
his law doth he meditate day and night.

And he shall be like a tree planted by the rivers
of water, that bringeth forth his fruit in his
season; his leaf also shall not wither; and
whatsoever he doeth shall prosper.

The ungodly are not so: but are like the chaff
which the wind driveth away.

Therefore the ungodly shall not stand in the
judgment, nor sinners in the congregation
of the righteous.

For the LORD knoweth the way of the
righteous: but the way of the ungodly shall
perish.

PSALM 1:1–6

I will sing of mercy and judgment: unto thee,
O Lord, will I sing.

I will behave myself wisely in a perfect way. O
when wilt thou come unto me? I will walk
within my house with a perfect heart.

I will set no wicked thing before mine eyes: I
hate the work of them that turn aside; it
shall not cleave to me.

A froward heart shall depart from me: I will
not know a wicked person.

Whoso privily slandereth his neighbour, him
will I cut off: him that hath an high look
and a proud heart will not I suffer.

PSALM 101:1–5

Better is the poor that walketh in his integrity,
than he that is perverse in his lips, and is a
fool.

PROVERBS 19:1

Blessed are the undefiled in the way, who walk
in the law of the LORD.
Blessed are they that keep his testimonies, and
that seek him with the whole heart.
They also do no iniquity: they walk in his
ways.
Thou hast commanded us to keep thy precepts
diligently.
O that my ways were directed to keep thy
statutes!
Then shall I not be ashamed, when I have
respect unto all thy commandments.
I will praise thee with uprightness of heart,
when I shall have learned thy righteous
judgments.
I will keep thy statutes: O forsake me not
utterly.

Psalm 119:1–8

A false balance is abomination to the LORD:
   but a just weight is his delight.
When pride cometh, then cometh shame: but
   with the lowly is wisdom.
The integrity of the upright shall guide them:
   but the perverseness of transgressors shall
   destroy them.

PROVERBS 11:1–3

A Heart of Wisdom

The days of our years are threescore years and
ten; and if by reason of strength they be
fourscore years, yet is their strength labour
and sorrow; for it is soon cut off, and we
fly away.
Who knoweth the power of thine anger? even
according to thy fear, so is thy wrath.
So teach us to number our days, that we may
apply our hearts unto wisdom.

PSALM 90:10–12

The fear of the LORD is the beginning of
wisdom: a good understanding have all
they that do his commandments: his praise
endureth for ever.

PSALM 111:10

How much better is it to get wisdom than
　　gold! and to get understanding rather to be
　　chosen than silver!

PROVERBS 16:16

Get wisdom, get understanding: forget it not;
　　neither decline from the words of my
　　mouth.
Forsake her not, and she shall preserve thee:
　　love her, and she shall keep thee.
Wisdom is the principal thing; therefore
　　get wisdom: and with all thy getting get
　　understanding.
Exalt her, and she shall promote thee: she shall
　　bring thee to honour, when thou dost
　　embrace her.
She shall give to thine head an ornament of
　　grace: a crown of glory shall she deliver to
　　thee.

PROVERBS 4:5–9

Keep my commandments, and live; and my
law as the apple of thine eye.
Bind them upon thy fingers, write them upon
the table of thine heart.
Say unto wisdom, Thou art my sister; and call
understanding thy kinswoman.

PROVERBS 7:2–4

Wisdom hath builded her house, she hath
hewn out her seven pillars:
She hath killed her beasts; she hath mingled her
wine; she hath also furnished her table.
She hath sent forth her maidens: she crieth
upon the highest places of the city,
Whoso is simple, let him turn in hither: as for
him that wanteth understanding, she saith
to him,
Come, eat of my bread, and drink of the wine
which I have mingled.
Forsake the foolish, and live; and go in the way
of understanding.

PROVERBS 9:1–6

But the wisdom that is from above is first pure, then peaceable, gentle, and easy to be intreated, full of mercy and good fruits, without partiality, and without hypocrisy.

JAMES 3:17

He that wasteth his father, and chaseth away
    his mother, is a son that causeth shame,
    and bringeth reproach.

PROVERBS 19:26

HOPE AND A FUTURE

But God, who is rich in mercy, for his great love wherewith he loved us,

Even when we were dead in sins, hath quickened us together with Christ, (by grace ye are saved;)

And hath raised us up together, and made us sit together in heavenly places in Christ Jesus:

That in the ages to come he might shew the exceeding riches of his grace in his kindness toward us through Christ Jesus.

EPHESIANS 2:4–7

Sing unto the LORD with thanksgiving; sing
   praise upon the harp unto our God:
Who covereth the heaven with clouds, who
   prepareth rain for the earth, who maketh
   grass to grow upon the mountains.
He giveth to the beast his food, and to the
   young ravens which cry.
He delighteth not in the strength of the horse:
   he taketh not pleasure in the legs of a man.
The LORD taketh pleasure in them that fear
   him, in those that hope in his mercy.
Praise the LORD, O Jerusalem; praise thy God,
   O Zion.
For he hath strengthened the bars of thy gates;
   he hath blessed thy children within thee.

PSALM 147:7–13

If ye then be risen with Christ, seek those things which are above, where Christ sitteth on the right hand of God.

Set your affection on things above, not on things on the earth.

For ye are dead, and your life is hid with Christ in God.

When Christ, who is our life, shall appear, then shall ye also appear with him in glory.

COLOSSIANS 3:1–4

For God hath not appointed us to wrath, but to obtain salvation by our Lord Jesus Christ,

Who died for us, that, whether we wake or sleep, we should live together with him.

Wherefore comfort yourselves together, and edify one another, even as also ye do.

1 THESSALONIANS 5:9–11

For as many as are led by the Spirit of God, they are the sons of God.

For ye have not received the spirit of bondage again to fear; but ye have received the Spirit of adoption, whereby we cry, Abba, Father.

The Spirit itself beareth witness with our spirit, that we are the children of God:

And if children, then heirs; heirs of God, and joint-heirs with Christ; if so be that we suffer with him, that we may be also glorified together. . . .

For we are saved by hope: but hope that is seen is not hope: for what a man seeth, why doth he yet hope for?

But if we hope for that we see not, then do we with patience wait for it.

ROMANS 8:14–17, 24–25

Blessed be the God and Father of our Lord Jesus Christ, which according to his abundant mercy hath begotten us again unto a lively hope by the resurrection of Jesus Christ from the dead,

To an inheritance incorruptible, and undefiled, and that fadeth not away, reserved in heaven for you,

Who are kept by the power of God through faith unto salvation ready to be revealed in the last time.

Wherein ye greatly rejoice, though now for a season, if need be, ye are in heaviness through manifold temptations:

That the trial of your faith, being much more precious than of gold that perisheth, though it be tried with fire, might be found unto praise and honour and glory at the appearing of Jesus Christ:

Whom having not seen, ye love; in whom, though now ye see him not, yet believing, ye rejoice with joy unspeakable and full of glory:

Receiving the end of your faith, even the salvation of your souls.

1 PETER 1.3–9

As Sisters in Faith We Focus on

A SISTER'S RELATIONSHIP WITH GOD

A SISTER'S RELATIONSHIP WITH HER FAMILY

A SISTER'S RELATIONSHIP WITH OTHERS

A SISTER'S RELATIONSHIP TO HER CAREER

A SISTER'S RELATIONSHIP WITH HERSELF

Notes

Notes

Notes

Notes

Notes

Notes

Notes